# CHINA

## Iris Teichmann

A⁺

**Smart Apple Media**

This book has been published in cooperation with Franklin Watts.

**Designer** Rita Storey
**Editor** Sarah Ridley
**Art Director** Jonathan Hair
**Editor-in-Chief** John C. Miles
**Picture Research** Diana Morris

**Picture credits**

Action Press/Rex Features: 22, 26. AP/Topfoto: 12.
Martin Benjamin/Image Works/Topfoto: 24. Mark Henley/Panos: 25.
Richard Jones/Sinopix/Rex Features: front cover tl, 23.
Lou Linwei/SinoPix/Rex Features: 20. Picturepoint/Topfoto: 9. Popperfoto: 13.
Qilai Shen/Panos: front cover b,1,18. SinoPix/Rex Features: 5, 21.
Sipa Press/Rex Features: front cover tr, 15, 16, 17, 27. Superbild/A1 Pix: 6, 19.
Superbild/Incolor/A1 Pix: 7, 11. The Travel Library/Rex Features: 14

Published in the United States by Smart Apple Media
2140 Howard Drive West, North Mankato, Minnesota 56003

Library of Congress Cataloging-in-Publication Data

Teichmann, Iris.
China / By Iris Teichmann.
p. cm. — (Countries in the news)
Includes bibliographical references and index.
ISBN-13: 978-1-59920-015-6
1. China—Juvenile literature. I. Title.

DS706.T45 2007
951—dc22          2006036146


9 8 7 6 5 4 3 2 1

.

# CONTENTS

**CHINA IS THE THIRD-BIGGEST COUNTRY IN THE WORLD,** *covering an area about twice the size of western Europe. It is home to around 1.3 billion people, roughly a fifth of the world's total population. China is a hugely diverse country, with mountains, plateaus, and deserts in the west, and low-level plains, huge river deltas, and hills in the east. Its most important river is the Yangtze (Chang Jiang), which flows from west to east across the country and supports more than 400 million people along its way.*

### ADMINISTRATION

China's capital is Beijing, which has been the center of political power for more than 500 years. Other important cities are Shanghai and Nanjing in the east; Chengdu, Chongqing, Wuhan, and Xian in central China; and Guangzhou in the southeast. The country is divided into 23 provinces and five self-governing regions (Tibet, Inner Mongolia, Ningxia, Xinjiang, and Guangxi) with their own local governments. The Chinese government administers Beijing, Tianjin, Shanghai, and Chongqing directly.

### CHINA'S POPULATION

More than 92 percent of the population is Han Chinese, or ethnic Chinese who live predominantly in central and eastern provinces. The rest of the population consists of at least 55 officially recognized minorities who live in the underdeveloped border regions. They include, among others, the Manchus, Tibetans, Uyghurs,

China's position in the world.

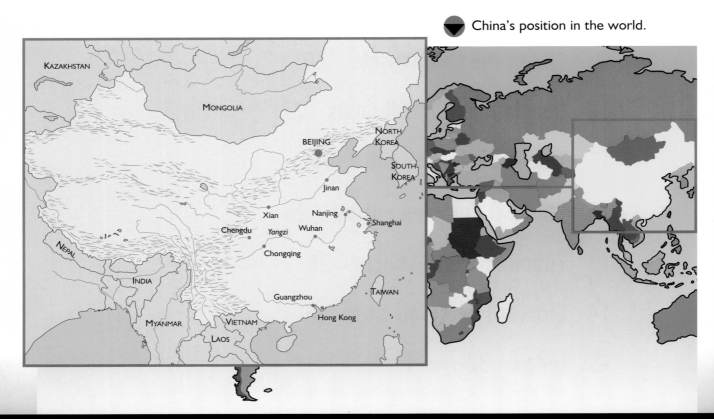

Mongolians, and Koreans. These groups have a strong culture and history of their own. There has been tension between minorities and the Han Chinese throughout history.

## THE RURAL POPULATION

When China came under Communist rule in 1949, about 90 percent of the population lived as farmers in the countryside. Rapid urban and economic development since the 1970s has changed this dramatically. The rural population has decreased to about 60 percent, and it is getting harder to make a living in the countryside. Millions of Chinese have migrated to cities in search of work.

## CHINA'S CHALLENGES

While people in the countryside are still relatively poor, a new middle class has emerged in the cities. They earn good money and are increasingly enjoying a better standard of living. They are more likely to be educated and know about the West, and may even have traveled. But for the Chinese population as a whole, coping with population pressures, the environmental impact of economic development, and the lack of political freedom are some of the biggest issues today.

China's growing population creates huge challenges for the country.

## KNOW YOUR FACTS

Despite China's size, only about 20 percent of the country is suitable for farming. This is not enough land to feed China's massive population, which is expected to reach one and a half billion in 2010. Also, the amount of farmland is decreasing as cities continue to grow. As a result, China has to buy more and more food, such as grain and rice, from other countries to be able to feed its growing population.

**CHINA HAS ONE OF THE WORLD'S LONGEST SURVIVING CIVILIZATIONS.** *As early as around 7000 B.C., people living in central and western China began to settle and make a living from farming the fertile soil. Excavations near Xian have revealed many items, such as pottery and tools, dating from this time.*

## SHANG DYNASTY

Until around 1500 B.C., different cultures and peoples had settled in different parts of China. Then the first line of ruling families (dynasties) began to spread power and influence across the country. The Shang dynasty is the first for which there is written evidence; it ruled until about 1050 B.C. Much of this evidence comes in the form of picture symbols inscribed onto animal bones used in religious ceremonies based around ancestor worship. The picture symbols developed into the written Chinese language we know today. Ancestor worship remains an important aspect of modern Chinese life.

## KNOW YOUR FACTS

Confucius (Kong Fuzi) was born in 551 B.C. and died in 478 B.C. He was a leading philosopher of his time, and his teachings have had a major influence on Chinese culture and society. He preached that for any man to be a good man, he would have to have the qualities of a learned scholar, be a true gentleman with good manners, and be a person who respects religion by worshipping his ancestors and respecting his parents. All of these, he would apply to every aspect of his daily life. Confucius felt that this was especially important for men who held positions of power.

## THE FIRST EMPEROR

Before 221 B.C., many groups of peoples lived in China, periodically fighting each other for power and influence. It was China's first emperor, Qin Shi, who was able to unify these groups and rule over a united land.

Qin Shi is remembered for ordering a network of roads to be built and for fortifying cities. Under his rule, the Chinese began to use a standard writing system and standard weights and measures, as well as coins for trading.

 Archaeologists have discovered many different types of bronze vessels, thought to be linked to Shang religious ceremonies.

 In 1974, 7,000 clay soldiers, known as the Terracotta Army, were discovered in Xian.

When Qin Shi died, he was buried with a vast army of clay figurines—the "Terracotta Army"—discovered by archaeologists in 1974. Since his death, China has remained one country. Qin Shi's achievements are so important in Chinese history that some historians think the word "China" actually comes from his name, "Qin" (pronounced "Chin").

## THE HAN DYNASTY

The Han dynasty (206 B.C.–A.D. 220) also had a lasting impact on Chinese history. The Han rulers were the first to build a sophisticated central and regional government system. People serving in government were instructed in the teachings of Confucius, whose influence was to last for thousands of years. Even

## GROUNDS FOR DEBATE

During the Qing dynasty (1644–1912), China flourished and became rich by selling its fine goods—silk, porcelain, and cotton—to other countries. In the meantime, many European countries wanted to sell their goods into China. However, China's rulers wished to keep the country isolated from outside influences and trade. In order to weaken Chinese power and open up trade, Britain smuggled the addictive drug opium into China. This led to many Chinese becoming addicted. The British then used their military might to force China to open up to the world.
What do you think of this policy?

when foreign cultures, such as the Mongols and the Manchus, invaded and ruled China in later times, they adopted Han culture, rather than forcing the Chinese to adopt theirs.

# 3 THE BIRTH OF THE PEOPLE'S REPUBLIC OF CHINA

**THE PRESENCE AND INFLUENCE OF WESTERN POWERS IN THE LATE 19TH CENTURY** *brought about massive changes to China and eventually led to a new political era and the end of imperial rule.*

## A TIME FOR CHANGE

Many intellectuals began to demand political change and to push for a new China without an emperor, where people would have more opportunity to improve their lives. These reformers were not just influenced by the West. China at that time had witnessed famine, and many people struggled to survive. China needed to change, not only politically, but also economically.

One of the main reformers, Sun Yatsen (Sun Zhongshan), had so much support from across China's population that he was able to proclaim the Republic of China in 1912. This move forced the last Chinese emperor, two-year-old Pu Yi, to abdicate.

Sun was not able to hold power for long. Two other political parties—the Communist Party and the Nationalist Party, also known as the Kuomintang—emerged. These two rivals would battle for power in China until 1949. This was a time of great political uncertainty as warlords fought each other in different parts of the country. The lack of a unified government allowed Japan to invade the region of Manchuria, in the north of China, in 1931.

## NATIONALIST VERSUS COMMUNIST

The Nationalist Party was led by the powerful military leader Chiang Kai-shek. It had its headquarters in Nanjing and wanted to establish a Western-style economy in China. The Communist Party, on the other hand, wanted to set up a Soviet-style Communist state with a state-run economy. With such differing political aims, the Communist Party split away and established its own stronghold.

When Nationalist forces attacked in 1934, the Communists were forced to flee into the countryside. This became known as the Long March. The Long March was in fact a series of marches undertaken by different Communist army groups. The longest march covered 4,970 miles (8,000 km) and lasted a year. It was led by Mao Zedong, who eventually became China's first president. In his group, 80,000 people set out, but only 10,000 made it to Yenan. The others died of exhaustion or illness, or they were killed because they lagged behind or tried to get away.

## CIVIL WAR

In 1937, Japan sent its forces farther into China. Despite their different political views, the Nationalists and the Communists were forced to join together to fight this foreign enemy. But when Japan surrendered at the end of World War II in 1945, the two rivals began an outright civil war. In the end, the

Communists, who had been regrouping and gaining support in the countryside, defeated the Nationalists, many of whom then joined the Communists. Chiang Kai-shek fled to the island of Taiwan with the rest of his supporters (see page 10), and Mao Zedong became the Communist Party's official leader. He proclaimed the People's Republic of China in Beijing on October 1, 1949.

This idealized government image shows Mao proclaiming the People's Republic of China on October 1, 1949.

## THE LONG MARCH, 1934

The Communist Party has long celebrated the Long March as an achievement, saying that it showed the strength and stamina of the Communist soldiers. In reality, it was beyond what even the Communist army could endure.

One Communist army officer described what it was like: "There was nowhere to escape the rain and no good sleep to be had, some sick and weak fell asleep and never woke up. Many suffered infected feet. As we left the base area farther and farther behind, some . . . deserted. The more obedient ones begged in tears to be let go."

# 4 TAIWAN: A CHINESE PROVINCE OR NOT?

**TO THE CHINESE GOVERNMENT, TAIWAN IS THE 23RD PROVINCE** *of the People's Republic of China. To the Taiwanese government, Taiwan is a country in its own right. The status of Taiwan, and whether it is part of China or not, is one of the most important unresolved issues in China today.*

## THE REPUBLIC OF CHINA

When Chiang Kai-shek fled the Communists and arrived in Taiwan in 1949, he claimed that his government in Taiwan was the true government of China and that it was only a matter of time before he would regain control of mainland China. At that time, Chiang had the support of the West, especially the United States, which stationed its navy along the Taiwanese coast to prevent the Communists from invading and claiming the island.

Chiang gave Taiwan the official name of the Republic of China, and many Western countries recognized it as the lawful government of the whole of China. It was even recognized by the United Nations. But in 1971, the UN voted to officially recognize the People's Republic of China as Taiwan's lawful government. Today, Taiwan is not legally recognized as an independent country by the international community, and it only has diplomatic ties with a handful of countries around the world.

## KNOW YOUR FACTS

Until the 17th century, Taiwan had no importance for imperial China. From 1642 to 1661, it was a Dutch colony. Then, in 1683, it fell under the control of the Qing dynasty. In 1895, Japan took control of Taiwan and developed its agriculture and improved transportation on the island.

## THE PEOPLES OF TAIWAN

The very first people to migrate to Taiwan were probably people from southeast Asia, but in the 17th century, Chinese from Fujian and Guangdong Province in southern China started to settle on the island in significant numbers. Descendants of these migrants still form the majority of Taiwan's population today; descendants of Chiang Kai-shek's followers only make up just over 10 percent.

## INTERNATIONAL FLASHPOINT

In the beginning, Chiang Kai-shek's government was not very popular. His son and successor, Jiang Jingguo, continued to rule as a military dictator. But since the 1970s, Taiwan has experienced considerable economic growth, making it one of the most successful economies on the continent of Asia.

The memorial to Sun Yatsen (see page 8) in Taipei, Taiwan's capital.

In the 1980s, democratic elections were introduced, ending military rule. In 2000, the Democratic Progressive Party, which wants Taiwan to become an independent and internationally recognized country, won the elections. Chen Shuibian became Taiwan's new president, ending the dominance of the Nationalist Party. Although Chen does not publicly declare Taiwan's independence, the Chinese government sees him as a threat and has indicated that it will use force if Taiwan decides to go its own way. The U.S. has promised support to Taiwan should China attack it.

## GROUNDS FOR DEBATE

China has always maintained that Taiwan is part of China. But in many ways, Taiwan is a country in its own right. It has its own political system, holds elections, has a constitution, and has its own armed forces. It is a member of the World Trade Organization and competes as a separate country in the Olympics. Most of the Taiwanese population has always identified itself as both Chinese and Taiwanese. However, this trend may change as the younger generation increasingly identifies itself as Taiwanese. Meanwhile, a political solution to Taiwan's status in the world is unlikely. What do you think?

**CHINA IS ONE OF THE FEW REMAINING COMMUNIST COUNTRIES IN TODAY'S WORLD.** *Recently, it has embraced a Western-style economy and tries to maintain good relations with the West. However, when Mao Zedong and the Communist Party took power in 1949, the country's policies and ideologies were very different.*

### NATIONALIZATION

After years of conflict, Mao wanted to bring stability and a modern economy to China. He thought that the way to do this was by creating powerful state industries and reforming agriculture. At that time, the vast majority of Chinese people were poor, landless farmers. Mao ordered that large farms be taken away from wealthy landowners and divided among the peasants. He hoped this would increase

Under Mao, large numbers of peasants became factory workers, like this welder.

agricultural output. At the same time, he organized the rapid expansion of industries in the cities.

His reforms brought some benefits. Some rural areas, especially those close to urban areas, saw the arrival of electricity, running water, and new technology to mechanize farming. But even though industrial output increased, the farmers simply could not produce enough food to feed the growing number of people who now worked in the industries in and around the cities. To solve this problem, Mao introduced the Great Leap Forward in 1958 (see panel) to try to make every village commune self-sufficient.

## THE GREAT LEAP FORWARD

The Great Leap Forward reorganized farming again, this time into village communes. This new method of working aimed to release some of the farmers into both large-scale building projects and small-scale rural industries, such as steel making. Without the correct raw materials, however, workers melted down farm tools and other metal items, and this produced worthless steel. It also meant that the same workers did not have time to farm their land properly. The results became catastrophic when poor harvests hit; around 30 million Chinese died of starvation in 1959 and 1960 alone.

## MAO STEPS DOWN

After the disaster that was the Great Leap Forward, Mao decided to retire. For the next seven years, his successors tried to rebuild China's economy. At the same time, tensions grew between China and the Soviet Union, which had been giving financial and expert help to China as a fellow Communist state.

## THE CULTURAL REVOLUTION

In 1966, Mao decided it was time to come out of retirement, and he regained power. He wanted to move China forward and leave all of the old ideas behind. His new big idea was the Cultural Revolution. This was in part a personality cult supported by millions of badges carrying Mao's face and millions of books containing Mao's quotations, the *Little Red Book*.

At the same time, Mao encouraged students in Beijing to attack their teachers and university staff for filling their heads with the wrong ideas. The students called themselves the Red Guards, and their actions turned into a violent purge across China. Intellectuals, writers, and artists were persecuted, tortured, and even killed. Schools and universities were closed, their teachers sent to work in the fields. Cultural relics and art were destroyed as Mao encouraged the Red Guards to stamp out old customs and old-fashioned ways of thinking. Millions of people died during these terrifying times.

Soldiers of the People's Liberation Army read in unison from Mao's *Little Red Book*.

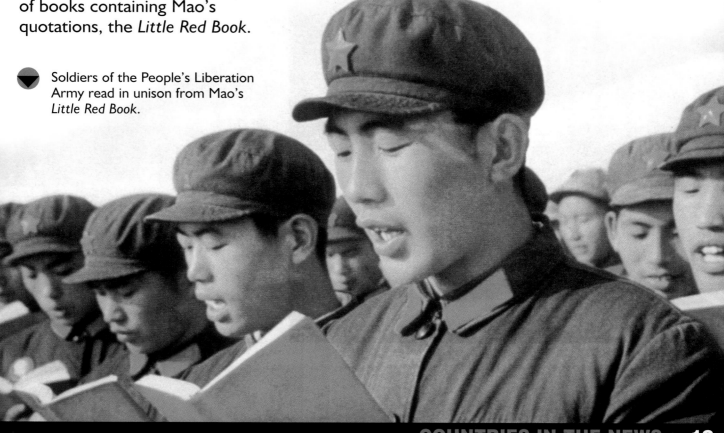

# KEY MOMENTS: CHINA'S MODERNIZATION

**AFTER MAO'S DEATH IN 1976, HIS SUCCESSOR, DENG XIAOPING,** *began to take steps to help China modernize. Deng wanted to improve China's economy and to get more foreign companies to invest in the country. This was a radical change from Mao's economic policies.*

## AGRICULTURE

Deng decided that collective farms alone could not feed China's huge population. He allowed farmers in the countryside to keep a private plot of land for themselves. The farmers continued to work on the large farming communes, but, for the first time, they could earn extra money by growing whatever they wanted on their private land and selling the produce at the local market. At the same time, the farming communes themselves could also sell any surplus and did not just have to rely on the government buying produce from them at set prices. This meant that farmers had some extra money to buy goods.

## SPECIAL ECONOMIC ZONES

Deng also declared that Zhuhai, Shenzhen, Shantou, and Xiamen along China's southern coast should become Special Economic Zones. If a foreign company set up a factory in any of these zones, it enjoyed special privileges such as reduced taxes. The government worked to improve the infrastructure in the zones, creating better roads, airports, and access to electricity and water supplies, as well as banks and hospitals. Foreign investment increased, and today there are Special Economic Zones all along China's coastline and farther inland along the Yangtze River.

These market traders at Kashgar sell the surplus produce of their small farms.

▲ Tanks roll into Tiananmen Square in 1989.

## THE TIANANMEN MASSACRE

In May 1989, a leading political figure in the Communist Party, Hu Yaobang, died. He was known for supporting moderate political reforms and encouraging an open dialogue with the West. When thousands of students gathered in Tiananmen Square in Beijing to hold a memorial service for him, the gathering turned into a peaceful demonstration for political reform in China. Over the next few days, many people joined the demonstration. This was too much for China's Communist government. On June 4, 1989, it ordered army tanks to roll into Tiananmen Square to disperse the demonstrators. The army opened fire, and many hundreds of people are thought to have died.

## CHINA'S ECONOMY TODAY

China's economy is mainly an export economy. Millions of Chinese workers in the Special Economic Zones assemble Western goods in factories set up by foreign companies. The goods are then exported to the West. Most experts agree that China's economic success is unlike any other. No other Communist regime has seen such economic transformation and development. As a result, many Chinese now enjoy a better income and can buy things they previously could not afford. But they still cannot choose and elect their government and therefore have no say in how their country is run.

**THE CHINESE COMMUNIST GOVERNMENT IS** *the biggest political party in the world. It does not allow other political parties and therefore has absolute control over its people. Even though the Chinese people have access to food, health services, education, and work opportunities, their political freedom is extremely restricted.*

## THE RIGHT TO JUSTICE

The Chinese leadership is very fearful of anyone who directly or indirectly criticizes, or in any other way presents a threat, to its absolute authority. Anyone doing so risks being detained, put under house arrest or in prison, or sent to a labor camp. Very often, lawyers themselves risk being put under surveillance or even arrested for defending individuals whom the government suspects of being dissidents.

Politicians listen and prepare to vote during a debate in the Chinese parliament's Great Hall.

## KNOW YOUR FACTS

At the top level of government is the Chinese Communist Party's Politburo, which controls the State Council. When the Politburo, for example, decides to declare a region in China a Special Economic Zone, the State Council will ensure that this happens.

Before this can happen, the National People's Congress has to formally approve the Politburo's decision. It usually does this, because it consists of unelected Communist Party members, recommended by the Chinese Communist Party itself. Any decisions made by the Communist Party's Politburo are therefore unlikely to be rejected by the National People's Congress.

The party structure goes all the way down to the village head in the countryside and the leader of the work unit in state-owned companies, who are usually also Communist Party members.

 U.S. president George W. Bush regularly meets with China's present leader, Hu Jintao.

The Tiananmen demonstrators of 1989 are still under house arrest or under constant surveillance by the police.

## FREEDOM OF SPEECH

The Chinese government also keeps a tight control over the media, art, and literature and can ban articles, plays, or books that it does not like. Even posting information on the Internet that the government does not agree with can lead to imprisonment. Internet cafés in China are required to monitor how their customers use the Internet. Many do not do this. The government shut down more than 47,000 Internet cafés in 2004 alone.

There is no doubt that life in China today is less restrictive than under Mao, but the Communist Party's control is still very strong, and it is unlikely that China's current political system will change in the near future.

## GROUNDS FOR DEBATE

Since Mao Zedong's death in 1976, China's relationship with the West has improved a great deal. Much of this has been because of China's desire to cooperate economically with other countries. Today, Western leaders meet regularly with China's leaders. When they do, they often try to raise the issue of human rights, but with no obvious results. Some argue that the West has in fact no real interest in improving human rights in China. They say that the West mainly wants to develop business opportunities in China and therefore does not want to annoy China's leaders. Others say that it is not really the responsibility of the West to help China open up politically—it is up to the Chinese people themselves. What do you think?

**WESTERNERS VISITING CHINA FOR THE FIRST TIME ARE USUALLY AMAZED** *at how developed China's cities are. In Beijing, Shanghai, Guangzhou, and other big cities, modern high-rise buildings are springing up everywhere, department stores have all the latest designer clothes, and Western fast-food and coffee shops have opened up.*

### CHINA'S MIDDLE CLASS

China's economic success has improved the life of many Chinese. There are an increasing number of Chinese who have found good jobs in the new hotels, banks, insurance companies, and other service

## KNOW YOUR FACTS

Some people in China do not have the freedom to live and work in different places in their own country. Although many rural people do move to the cities for work, these migrant workers are not allowed to register to live in a city. This system was set up by the Chinese government in 1953 to try to get people to stay in their villages. Without a city registration permit, a rural migrant gets lower wages and has to pay more for schooling and other benefits.

Old and new—traditional buildings give way to skyscrapers in Shanghai.

Many traditional aspects of city life remain. Here, people perform outdoor exercises.

and leisure companies that have gained a foothold in China's cities. This emerging middle class has values and goals that are very different from those of their parents and grandparents. Whereas their parents under Mao Zedong had to accept the job that was given to them by the government, China's new middle class usually consists of well-educated people who have chosen their jobs and enjoy the things their new lifestyle can bring.

## THE UNDERCLASS

But life has not improved for everyone in the cities. In some of the more populous cities, such as Beijing and Shanghai, competition for jobs among the many migrant workers from the countryside (see panel) is fierce, and many are left without jobs. Some feel forced to accept jobs with dangerous working conditions

## GROUNDS FOR DEBATE

Some experts say that China's economic success cannot continue because it relies too much on the presence of foreign companies and exporting goods abroad. Many people would lose their jobs if these foreign companies moved away from China. Others say that it would be better to turn the state-run industries into private companies that could produce better, more competitive goods. More Chinese would then be willing to buy Chinese, rather than foreign, goods. What do you think?

and long working hours. More and more Chinese workers are also losing their jobs because many of the state-run companies are closing down, as they are poorly run and inefficient. Without the old security of a job for life, unemployment is rising, and many fear that this could lead to an increase in social tension and even crime.

# 9 LIFE IN THE COUNTRYSIDE

Many rural dwellers seek work on the huge building projects in China's booming cities.

**EVEN THOUGH CHINA HAS DEVELOPED** *enormously economically since the late 1970s, this kind of growth has not happened everywhere in China.*

Areas in central, western, and northern China have in fact developed very little. These are places that are difficult to reach and where it is often hard to grow much food. The population tends to be much more spread out, making it challenging to set up industries. The people who live here are among the poorest in China.

## FARMERS

For farmers in the countryside, it has become more difficult to make ends meet in recent years. Although farmers are permitted to sell their produce at open markets, they earn less money from the food they sell to the Chinese government, which does not pay as much anymore for the items it buys from them. At the same time, in some rural areas, Communist Party officials are known to get farmers to pay more taxes to them than they should. Corruption among these local officials is one of the biggest problems in China.

## THE FLOATING POPULATION

Since there are no other jobs in the countryside, more and more people travel to the nearest city to find work. If they cannot get a job there, they often travel even longer distances to find work in one of the big cities in central or eastern China. Around 150 to 200 million people are thought to be on the move to find a job in this way. They are known as the floating population.

The Chinese government knows that one way of addressing some of the problems in its growing cities is by improving the quality of life for people in the countryside. It has therefore recently said that it will reduce taxes for farmers to help them maximize their income. It also wants to encourage people to stay in the villages by promising to pay for children's education for at least nine years.

## KNOW YOUR FACTS

Hundreds of thousands of Chinese, mostly from southern China, are thought to be working abroad and sending money back home. This money has helped boost the income of their families. But this massive migration has also separated families. In some villages, all of the people of working age have gone overseas.

 Hard life—a farmer works his small plot of land in the countryside.

# 10 DEVELOPMENT AT ALL COSTS

**CHINA'S ECONOMIC SUCCESS** *is so great that experts say it will soon become the biggest economy in the world and even overtake the U.S. But the fast economic development comes at a price. Many environmental experts are concerned that China is turning into the biggest polluter on the planet.*

## THIRST FOR ENERGY

China needs enormous amounts of energy to drive its expanding industries and to provide an electricity supply to its vast population. It continues to rely heavily on coal for energy—but burning coal emits carbon dioxide into the atmosphere. Carbon dioxide is a gas that, in huge amounts, contributes to global warming.

The Three Gorges Dam will produce large amounts of electricity, but at what cost?

## GROUNDS FOR DEBATE

To help meet the growing demand for energy, the Chinese government began building the Three Gorges Dam in Hubei Province in 1994. It will be the biggest hydroelectric dam in the world when completed in 2009 and will produce electricity equivalent to 19 nuclear power stations.

The project involves diverting water from the Yangtze River into a 350-mile-long (560 km) reservoir between the cities of Yichang and Chongqing, which will also flood the scenic Three Gorges Valley. Two million people will lose their homes and livelihoods, many archaeological sites will be lost, and wildlife and the environment in the area will be affected. The dam will produce renewable energy, but at a cost. Is it worth it? What do you think?

## GROUNDS FOR DEBATE

The thousands of cars now in Chinese cities create huge air pollution and smog problems.

At the same time, more and more people in China can afford cars and motorcycles that guzzle oil and create air pollution. In many cities, the air quality is so poor that many Chinese wear masks to protect themselves from air pollution. Even the Chinese government has admitted that 5 of the 10 most polluted cities in the world are in China.

### POPULATION DEMANDS

But it's not just the need for energy that causes environmental problems. China's population of one and a half billion continues to grow. This means an increased consumption of food and other resources, which in turn increases waste, uses up more land, and produces more pollution. Even though the Chinese

China's environmental problems are no different than those in the West, and many people argue that the Chinese are simply becoming used to a lifestyle that Westerners have enjoyed for many years. Most agree that something needs to be done but disagree about which area to focus on. Some say that China, like the West, needs to urgently invest in renewable energy sources such as wind and solar power. They argue that the West can help by only allowing goods that meet strict environmental standards to be imported from China.

government is trying to create more awareness about reducing and recycling waste and using environmentally friendly products, environmental issues are still rarely discussed in the media.

# 11 THE ONE-CHILD FAMILY

**DURING THE 20TH CENTURY,** *China's population increased alarmingly. Worried about how to feed such a large population, the government passed a law in 1979 that allowed couples just one child—the one-child policy.*

This policy has been very unpopular, especially in rural areas where children are needed to help on the family farm and to look after the parents in their old age.

To implement this policy, officials in the past offered financial rewards to couples who had just one child. They also punished couples who did not conform by lowering their social benefits or even putting them out of a job. Some women, pregnant with a second child, were forced to have abortions. Today, this policy has been relaxed slightly.

## KNOW YOUR FACTS

For a Chinese family, a boy is better than a girl because boys can better help farm the land and look after the parents. A girl will eventually move to her husband's family when she marries and will also be expected to bring a dowry (large money gift) with her. So not only does a girl cost parents money, she will also not be around to bring in an income. Especially in poor rural areas, baby girls are often given away or the birth is not reported so that the parents can try for a son. Some baby girls are even killed.

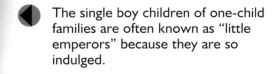
The single boy children of one-child families are often known as "little emperors" because they are so indulged.

## MORE BOYS THAN GIRLS

One result of the policy is that over the last 30 years, many more baby boys have been born than girls. Now that these boys have grown up, they are finding it increasingly difficult to find a partner. There is evidence that the situation has gotten so bad that women are being kidnapped and sold to men for marriage.

The one-child policy has been effective in that couples today have, on average, one and a half children, compared to six children in the 1970s. However, in the cities, many young professionals are enjoying their new lifestyle and often choose not to have children at all. Experts think that because of this, China's population will in fact start to decline sometime in the mid-21st century.

## GROUNDS FOR DEBATE

The one-child policy has completely changed family life in China. Whereas most families had 6 children 30 years ago, today they have an average of 1.5. With only one child to focus on, the single child is often spoiled and also put under a lot of pressure to do well at school and work. Without brothers and sisters with whom to grow up, many children are not learning consideration toward others. Psychologists worry about what effects the policy will have on Chinese society. Will the family break down? Who will look after the elderly?

Chinese baby girls are frequently given up for adoption, often to childless Western couples.

**WESTERN COUNTRIES HAVE TAKEN** *more than 100 years to industrialize, while China is developing much more quickly and has become a major economic power within only three to four decades. This has meant massive changes for Chinese society.*

While more and more Chinese can now afford to buy washing machines, televisions, and even cars, the vast majority are still relatively poor and have to work hard to make ends meet. Some fear that the gap between the poor and the better-off will get wider unless the government tries to improve the situation for farmers in the countryside and tackle unemployment in the cities.

## BORDER REGIONS

The lack of development and opportunities is particularly acute in the border regions, where most of China's

## KNOW YOUR FACTS

Tibet in western China has a unique culture, focused around Buddhism. Until China invaded Tibet in 1950, Tibet was of no political interest to anyone. When the Tibetans revolted against Chinese control in 1959, the revolt was brutally suppressed, and the Tibetan leader, the Dalai Lama, fled for safety to India, where he still lives in exile. Tibet still has a regional government, but the Communist Party in Beijing has removed all Tibetans from office and put Chinese officials in their place.

ethnic minorities live. The Chinese army is heavily present in Tibet and Xinjiang, as rebellions at the local level continue to occur, not just because of the lack of

China is Westernizing quickly, as shown by the presence of multinational companies.

Lots of luxury cars for sale are an indicator of just how much China has changed.

development there, but also because many Tibetans and Uyghurs want their provinces to be independent.

As China has developed much more quickly economically than the West, it has had less time to deal with the growing environmental impact. Access to doctors is relatively good in eastern, central, and southern China, and life expectancy in China has increased ever since the Communist Party came to power. But faced with serious water and air pollution, more and more people are becoming ill with respiratory diseases and cancer. China's current healthcare system is stretched, and the government is trying to find more ways to put money into it and make it more accessible across China.

## POLITICAL CHANGE?

It is likely that as environmental and social problems become more pressing, more Chinese will rebel against the government and openly support a change from a one-party political system to a more democratic alternative. Already, the Chinese government has to deal with local demonstrations in rural areas where people have become angry, not only about the lack of opportunities, but also about corrupt village party officials.

Change may also come from those young city-dwelling professionals who are working hard to earn money and improve their lifestyle. They may eventually become disillusioned with the government and want to have a say in who is running their country.

**7000 B.C.** First farming settlements begin in central and western China.

**1500 B.C.** The Shang dynasty establishes itself. Its people practice ancestor worship and develop a writing system and bronze technology.

**1045 B.C.** The Zhou dynasty sets up a government bureaucracy and develops basic social and political ideals.

**481–221 B.C.** The Zhou dynasty collapses, and many independent kingdoms fight for power and authority. During this time, China's most influential philosopher, Confucius, lives.

**221–210 B.C.** China's first emperor, Qin Shi Huangdi, unites China.

**206 B.C.–A.D. 220** The Han dynasty rules and sets up a sophisticated government system across the country based on the values and ideas of the philosopher Confucius.

**A.D. 141** Emperor Wu reigns. He expands the Han empire into Central Asia and makes Confucianism the official government moral code.

**A.D. 220–589** The kingdom is divided, and different regimes rule in the north and the south. Buddhism and Taoism become the dominant religions.

**618–907** China's golden age—the Tang dynasty is a strong and vibrant dynasty. This is the age of poetry, Buddhism, landscape paintings, and other art.

**960–1279** The Sung dynasty sets up a Confucian scholar-official government. Civil servants have to pass exams to serve. Trade develops, and towns grow.

**1272–1368** Mongols invade China and set up the Yuan dynasty but continue to develop Chinese cultural traditions.

**1368–1644** The Chinese regain control and establish the Ming dynasty. They move the capital to Beijing in 1421. Poetic and painting traditions develop further. This is also the age of novels.

**1644** The Manchus conquer China and set up the Qing dynasty. China's economy and trade grow. This is a time of extensive scholarship, with the emperors commissioning encyclopedias.

**1839–42** First Opium War between China and Britain is followed by another Opium War in 1856–60.

**1894–95** China is defeated by the Japanese in the Sino-Japanese War.

**1912** The Qing dynasty collapses, and the Republic of China is proclaimed by Sun Yatsen.

**1912–49** The Nationalists and Communists fight for power in China, while Japan invades China during World War II.

**1949** Mao Zedong proclaims the People's Republic of China in Tiananmen Square in Beijing, while the Nationalists continue the Republic of China government in Taiwan.

**1950** China invades Tibet.

**1958–60** Mao Zedong launches the Great Leap Forward, a five-year economic plan to drive industrial production. Agriculture is severely limited, and millions of people starve to death.

**1966–76** Mao Zedong tries to regain his authority and popularity with a political and ideological campaign, the Cultural Revolution. It aims to develop people's revolutionary spirit but causes widespread social and economic unrest.

**1971** The UN officially recognizes the People's Republic of China as China's legitimate government.

**1976** Mao Zedong dies.

**1977** Deng Xiaoping becomes leader and helps China open up toward the West and modernize its economy. Private businesses, foreign investment, and the market economy are encouraged.

**1989** The government brutally suppresses a week-long demonstration by students demanding rehabilitation of former Communist Party General Secretary Hu Yaobang and democratic reforms. Officially, 200 demonstrators die, but many think the number is much higher.

**1995** China carries out missile tests and military exercises off the coast of Taiwan during Taiwan's presidential elections.

**1997** Deng Xiaoping dies, and Hong Kong is handed back to China by the British.

**2001** China joins the World Trade Organization.

**2005** Taiwan's National Party leader, Lien Chan, visits China. It is the first meeting between Nationalist and Communist leaders since 1949. China passes a law that says it will use military force if Taiwan declares independence from mainland China.

# BASIC FACTS

**LOCATION:** East Asia, bordering Mongolia in the north; North Korea in the east; Vietnam, Laos, Burma, Bhutan, Nepal in the south and southwest; and India, Pakistan, Tajikistan, Kyrgyzstan, and Kazakhstan in the west.

**TOTAL LAND AREA:** 3,600,000 square miles (9,326,000 sq km).

**LANGUAGES:** Mandarin (standard Chinese and the official government language), Cantonese, Wu (Shanghai dialect), Minbei and Minnan (dialects spoken in Fuzhou and also Taiwan), and a number of other dialects and minority languages.

**CURRENCY:** Yuan (Chinese dollar), but also called Renminbi ("the currency of the people").

**LITERACY RATE:** Very high—just over 95 percent of men over 15 and 86 percent of women over 15 (2002 estimate).

**RELIGIONS:** No official religion, but Taoism, Buddhism, and Confucianism are the most popular religions.

**ETHNIC GROUPS:** Han Chinese just over 91 percent; the remainder are Manchu, Tibetans, Uyghurs, Mongolians, Koreans, Miao, and others.

**INDUSTRIES:** Mining, iron, steel, arms and machinery, textiles, petroleum, chemicals, consumer products such as shoes, toys, and electronics, food processing and transportation equipment, telecommunications.

**AGRICULTURE:** Rice, wheat, potatoes, corn, peanuts, tea, millet, barley, apples, cotton, oilseed, pork, fish.

**LABOR FORCE:** 791.4 million (2005 estimate).

**TRANSPORTATION:** 472 airports, 44,675 miles (71,900 km) of railways, 1,124,575 miles (1,809,830 km) of roads, and 75,530 miles (121,560 km) of waterways.

**Buddhism**  A religion that spread from India to China and says that suffering in life stops when we do not wish for anything.

**Colony**  An area of land, or a country, separate from the mother country but ruled by it.

**Commune**  A group of people working together, usually in the countryside.

**Communism**  A political and economic system in which the state owns all property. Individuals are provided with work, food, and housing.

**Consumerism**  An economy or lifestyle based on buying more and more goods.

**Corruption**  The abuse of power or an important position to make money.

**Dictatorship**  A government in which one person, usually backed by one party, rules the country without having been elected.

**Dynasty**  A succession of rulers from the same family line.

**Economy**  The organization of a country's money and resources.

**Excavation**  Digging deep into the ground to find remains of people, settlements, or art from a long time ago.

**Export**  Selling goods or services to a buyer outside your own country.

**Global warming**  The rising temperature of Earth's atmosphere partly caused by the buildup of gases such as carbon dioxide.

**Human rights**  A set of rights that everyone in the world should be entitled to, such as the right to free speech and the right to education.

**Hydroelectric power**  Electricity generated by water power.

**Ideology**  A group of thoughts, beliefs, and ideas put together.

**Labor camp**  A secure place where people convicted of crimes or accused of opposing the government may be sent and forced to work.

**Middle class**  People with a good, but not large, income that enables them to buy many goods and services and lead a comfortable life.

**Opium**  A strong drug made from poppies.

**Propaganda**  Information that is spread among society to support a belief or a cause.

**Soviet Union** The first communist state, which consisted of Russia and much of eastern Europe and central Asia. It lasted from 1922 until 1991.

**Tax** A charge made by a government.

**Trade** The buying and selling of goods and services.

**United Nations** An international organization bringing together representatives from 189 countries. It was set up in 1945 to uphold peace through international cooperation.

**Warlord** A military leader who controls local areas in a country.

**World Trade Organization** An international organization in which member countries agree to freely trade in services, such as banking and healthcare.

**World War II** The biggest world conflict in history. It involved most of the world's countries from 1939 until 1945.

# USEFUL WEB SITES

**http://www.info.gov.hk**
The Hong Kong government's official site.

**http://english.gov.cn/index.htm**
The official site of the government of the People's Republic of China.

**http://www.china.org.cn**
The China Internet Information Center, containing comprehensive information about China.

**http://www.chinasite.com**
A useful directory of Web sites on anything related to China and the Chinese.

**www.state.gov**
This U.S. government site contains detailed country reports, including China, Hong Kong, and Taiwan.

**http://www.chinadaily.com.cn**
A Chinese newspaper published in English.

**http://www.hrw.org/doc/ ?t=asia&c=china**
Detailed information about the human rights situation in China by Human Rights Watch, a nongovernmental organization.

**Note to parents and teachers:**
Every effort has been made to ensure that the Web sites in this book are suitable for children, that they are of the highest educational value, and that they contain no inappropriate or offensive material. However, because of the nature of the Internet, it is impossible to guarantee that the contents of these sites will not be altered. We strongly advise that Internet access be supervised by a responsible adult.